T0146805

TRADE SECRETS OF THE SUCCESSFUL HAIRSTYLIST

THE SUCCESSFUL HAIRSTYLIST'S PROVEN TECHNIQUES FOR MAKING A LOT MORE MONEY WHILE WORKING FEWER HOURS!

ALLISON BRIDGES

iUNIVERSE, INC.
BLOOMINGTON

Trade Secrets of the Successful Hairstylist
The Successful Hairstylist's Proven Techniques for Making A
Lot More Money While Working Fewer Hours!

The information, ideas, and suggestions in this book are not intended to render professional advice. Before following any suggestions contained in this book, you should consult your personal accountant or other financial advisor. Neither the author nor the publisher shall be liable or responsible for any loss or damage allegedly arising as a consequence of your use or application of any information or suggestions in this book.

iUniverse Star

an iUniverse, Inc. imprint

iUniverse books may be ordered through booksellers or by contacting:

iUniverse
1663 Liberty Drive
Bloomington, IN 47403
www.iuniverse.com
1-800-Authors (1-800-288-4677)

Because of the dynamic nature of the Internet, any Web addresses or links contained in this book may have changed since publication and may no longer be valid. The views expressed in this work are solely those of the author and do not necessarily reflect the views of the publisher, and the publisher hereby disclaims any responsibility for them.

ISBN: 978-1-938908-08-8 (sc)
ISBN: 978-1-938908-09-5 (ebk)

Library of Congress Control Number: 2012913891

Printed in the United States of America

iUniverse rev. date: 7/26/2012

100% Money-Back Guarantee

**You will increase your sales within thirty days
of using this book!
Or you will receive a full refund from me personally!**

This book is dedicated to
increasing *your* income!

Special Thanks and Gratitude to
Tim, Gwyneth, Lucas, Logan,
Maryanne, Ann, and everyone at Evolutions

CONTENTS

CHAPTER ONE

CHANGING THE WAY YOU LOOK AT YOUR BUSINESS

MORE MONEY AND MORE FREE TIME!

The financial life of a hairstylist is like a roller coaster. During the peak season of December, you're so busy you feel like you can't catch your breath; you're running around like crazy, and cash is being handed out left and right. Then the reality of January hits, and hardly anyone is calling for an appointment. For years I rode the roller coaster because I thought I had to. I thought the money was cyclical and clients rode the seasons. When things were good, they were very good; and when they were bad, they would pass—at least I hoped so.

Through this book I will impart the tools I developed to finally get off this roller coaster. I will guide you through concrete steps you can begin using immediately that will help you get the results you need. Through my experiences, both working as a hairstylist and owning my own salon, I have learned valuable lessons that will accelerate your career to a new level of success whether

1

you are a seasoned hairstylist or a recent beauty school graduate.

Like so many stylists, I began my hairstyling career as an apprentice. My job required a four-hour commute five days a week to the Vidal Sassoon salon located in the Union Square section of lower Manhattan. As is the policy at Vidal Sassoon, I needed to pick which department I wanted to work in and choose whether I wanted to specialize in cutting hair or applying color. I decided to go into cutting.

During the week, I paid my dues. I stood ten feet away from the stylist I was assigned to, and my job was to retrieve whatever it was that stylist needed. I cleaned brushes every morning, swept floors, laundered towels and robes—all the things apprentices experience before they go on the floor.

Once a week on Mondays, when the salon was quiet, we received training so we could move up to junior stylists. This involved meticulously learning and being tested on six trademark Sassoon haircuts. This proved to be the most difficult for me because I found that I was a lot more interested in the other aspects of running a salon, rather than learning the cutting details of a Sassoon haircut. So unfortunately my attention was lost pretty quickly.

During the rest of the week, though, I proved to be a model employee, taking care of clients and keeping the shop clean. Gretchen, the head manager, noticed my take-charge attitude, that I naturally supervised the other apprentices and told them what to do when things were not being done properly. My co-workers were probably less than thrilled, but Gretchen increasingly found she could trust me to follow through on whatever job she gave me. Soon I was the go-to girl when any department in the salon needed a fill-in. I would help out at the front desk, booking appointments and checking out clients. They would use me to organize and take care of the inventory. I even worked one year at the display booth at the International Beauty Show selling Sassoon products. All of this was a lot of fun; I enjoyed being exposed to these different areas of the hair business.

I had been working at Sassoon for a year and a half when one of the stylists was let go. I was asked to call and reassign her clients to another stylist. When I finished that task, Gretchen looked up at me from the reports she was examining, smiled, and said "Nice job. Maybe you should think about going for a managerial position." Just like that, she went right back to her reading. Well, she had really given me something to think about. You could definitely say I had a managerial attitude, but I have to admit I didn't have a natural talent for hairdressing. My Monday training sessions weren't going so well because I wasn't making them my top priority. I had been at Sassoon for a year and a half, and I was only up to the second haircut out of six. Being a manager meant long hours in the office and total responsibility for all the payroll hours and paychecks, keeping track of twenty-five to thirty employees, overseeing everyone's schedules, keeping up with all the inventory—and still taking haircutting clients every day.

I started asking the hairstylists that were already on the floor how long it took them to finish their training. Most of them told me a year to a year and a half, which put my own training into perspective. If I continued moving through the curriculum at my present snail's pace, it would take me four and a half years to get on to the floor, plus whatever time it would take to work my way up from junior stylist to stylist to senior stylist to assistant manager and eventually head manager.

Having been distracted by all the other jobs I had taken on in the salon, I was embarrassed that I had become so negligent about learning what I needed to move forward as a stylist. Whether I was just impatient or impulsive, I decided I didn't want to wait. Two weeks later I jumped ship after my friend Maryanne got me an interview at the local salon where she worked, only a few minutes drive from the apartment I shared with my husband, Tim. I don't know if the owner was more impressed with my fancy Sassoon credentials or my persuasive manner, but he gave me a chair. I was so excited leaving that interview! I finally had a chair, and it hadn't been so hard to do after all. That is, until I realized I only actually knew how to do two haircuts and had absolutely no color experience at all.

It probably won't surprise you that during the first six months that I was on the floor, most of my clients walked out with a bob or a one-length trim. Over the next two years, my very patient friend, Maryanne, taught me color skills. I had built a small clientele, and I was doing okay. My income was very much hostage to the season, just like many of the other stylists in this salon. My gross sales total each week was between five hundred and nine hundred dollars, but I was also always stuck with several no-shows each month, especially during the slow seasons, and a good portion of each day was spent waiting for my next client to show up.

Then one Saturday afternoon I had a revelation. I was waiting for a notoriously flaky client that had stood me up the month prior. I hung around the salon between appointments for about three hours waiting for her time to roll around, hoping there might be a walk-in client or a last-minute appointment, but I had no such luck. As a commission-paid stylist, I was allowed to come and go pretty much as I pleased, so when clients don't show, you just don't get paid, and the time that gets wasted is yours. Well, I think you can pretty much guess what happened: four-thirty, four-thirty five, four-forty, damn it! I had been stood up again by the same client. I threw my scissors, brushes, and blow-dryer in a bag and went home. During the short car ride home, I became really angry: not only was I losing my income, but the client didn't have any respect for my time.

I felt frustrated and stymied, tired of just being average, but I didn't know how to build a better clientele. Sassoon had been a great place for learning haircuts and self-discipline, and Maryanne was great for teaching me color, but a huge chunk of the puzzle was missing for me. I wondered, after you pass the state boards, why can't the proctor give you a book as you walk out the door along the lines of *A Professional Hairstylist's Guide*—an insiders' handbook—that explains how to actually make money in this industry and how things work out in the real world.

I arrived home, and I stewed the rest of the weekend. I didn't know what I was going to do to get where I wanted to go in life. In the current state of my career, I felt like I was just wasting my time week after week, never getting anywhere, with no end in sight. The years of busy-slow-busy-slow seasonal cycles were driving me crazy and making a mess of my finances. I couldn't be confident of what I would bring home week to week, and I knew it was time to break this cycle.

By Tuesday morning, something had clicked. I believe people can transform their lives at any age, and it comes with the realization that they are in charge of their lives. No one else controls our decisions unless we give them permission to, and ultimately the way to deal with our circumstances is completely up to ourselves.

That day I made the decision to own my career and not blame the seasons, the industry, my lack of information, or dissatisfied and cranky clients for my not being successful. No more. From then on I would honor my sanity, income, and financial security and begin the very next day to make the changes that would benefit my career. At the top of that list, I would take steps to secure a steady income for the entire year, no matter what.

One of the most important things I noticed while working at Vidal Sassoon is that they were busy year-round, not just during holidays and weekends. So were a few stylists at my current salon. So I knew it was possible for me to do the same thing if only I could figure out what was different about them and what was preventing me from taking my career to the same place.

Wednesday morning came, and back to work I went. I started paying more attention to the workings of this business and to the patterns of my clients and theirs. That was a turning point for me. I recognized I had to stop doing the easiest and fastest thing and begin to mimic all the things that the busy stylists were doing. More importantly, I saw I had to drop the bad habits

I had picked up from the not-so-great stylists. I am embarrassed to admit it now, but those ranged from using dirty brushes filled with other clients' hair to arriving late to work when my client was already there waiting for me to not looking the part of a professional stylist as far as my hair and makeup were concerned. Eventually I was able to attract a "better" type of client.

I also took every class I could afford to polish my skills, especially color classes. By broadening my ideas on color techniques, I was able to serve a much wider age range of clients, especially the younger clients who crave more creative techniques. Your local beauty supplier or hair color sales representative will have information about classes. Haircutting and coloring DVDs can also be a helpful resource.

So I began making more money, and I was happy, even though my time was still not completely maximized. A few of my lazy ways *still* lingered, but I was much better and I enjoyed seeing the results. The most important task still ahead was to figure out the right type of client to put my energy into, and I did this by watching the front desk when clients were checking out. I started to pay close attention to whether or not they booked their next appointment and how soon they came back in. I meandered along through a pregnancy and maternity leave; and when I decided that I wanted to go back to work, I knew that I might as well work in my own business. I guess Gretchen was right about me becoming a salon manager after all!

I purchased my first salon May 1, 2006. I started looking at the classified ads in April and found two salons for sale. I looked at the first one and quickly realized that everything needed to be replaced. The owner had also represented that this salon was grossing $200,000 a year in sales when they had barely anything on the books, as well as that, a four-by-four-foot box of dusty glass retail shelves was a cash cow. I may have been naïve but not that naïve. On the other hand, the second salon was a winner—the chairs, sinks, flooring, and stations were all newly replaced, and the owner wanted out as fast as possible. Less than a month later, I had a $60,000 home equity loan out on my house and was the proud new owner of a "thriving" salon. The business had been under the same ownership for seventeen years. Savvy new business owner that I thought I was, I was sure this transition would be a piece of cake since this was a turnkey situation. I fully believed the transition would be smooth. Right.

When I began looking into the business, I saw that the prices for services were posted on the wall behind the reception area. Haircutting and blow-dry services were 15 to 50 percent lower than what I usually charged, but I did not think to question them. The coloring services seemed to be right on par with what I currently charged, so I wasn't worried. And I knew that the owner hadn't raised any prices in over three years, so I figured the time was right to increase the prices a little bit here and there to get some of them closer to what I usually charged. After three years, I didn't think the clients would mind.

Well, I was wrong. During the first week in the salon, I discovered that the prices on the wall didn't mean anything, that each client had been given a different price and some were significantly below the already low prices listed, and that nothing was on record. I also learned the former owner was giving away free blow-dries with color services, essentially rewarding clients who skipped their haircut. And then I found out I was pregnant with my second child. Well, I was no longer just meandering along anymore. There would be no more daily trips to the park or Baby Einstein videos in the afternoon this time. This was a serious situation to be in: talk about motivation to fix things fast.

Now that I was responsible for the business's loans and expenses, including my second mortgage, staff salaries, and bringing in a steady income for my family, I began working around the clock. Every waking hour I was working—if it wasn't physically in the shop, it was mentally preparing for the next day. During my first maternity leave, I started a part-time housecleaning business to gain some business experience and to try something new. Primarily I managed schedules and dealt with customers, so it didn't take much time during the day, although I did have to be available to this business as well. So I knew I couldn't just run away again, like I had at Sassoon. This time my house was on the line, and I had children depending on me.

My first year in business was definitely tense. This was the point when I knew I needed to learn to be a serious business owner and do it fast. The casual attitude I had taken before was absolutely not good enough any more. "No more excuses" became my little internal voice, and I still hear it today. Eventually I sold the housecleaning business. I was also fortunate enough to have been given some excellent business advice at just the right time by Ginger, a former business consultant and one of my very good salon clients. She took pity on my little fledgling operation and one night gave me a crash course in operating a successful business.

This "new" information, combined with all of the great information I had collected over the years, transformed my business. I analyzed and utilized almost every piece of advice or observation I had ever gathered and poured them out on paper over many late nights while preparing for staff meetings throughout the first year. It was essentially like writing my business plan, something I had not done prior to purchasing the salon. To their credit and benefit, my stylists put up with the changes I made constantly and my consistent nudging and have transformed themselves completely. We have gone from a discount hair salon to the top salon in our area. We have the most professional staff around and carry only the best product lines. Our client base is triple that of the original business, and our sales are also 75 percent higher than what they were when I first took over—all within two years. Evolutions Hair Salon is now a salon that I am truly proud to own.

Putting this new information to work for me has taken my life as a stylist/business owner to a whole new level. I have lots of time with my children now that my time in the salon is only about twenty-five hours a week. My personal average sales week has more than doubled to $2,000, and I know that my income will be steady year-round because my appointment book is always consistently booked solid at *least* six to seven weeks in advance. Many of my clients prebook for the entire year now because they don't want to lose their favorite time slot.

Every single part of my workday is now completely maximized. I am making great money just about every minute I am in the salon, and that is no accident. What follows is how I did it. You can do it too.

THE SECRET IS THE ELITE CLIENT

Maryanne and Kerry were the two top stylists in my old salon, so I paid most of my attention to what their clients did when checking out. When I had a lot of time on my hands, I would spend my time waiting at the reception area rather than the back room so I could have more opportunities to learn about the front desk and be the first to get any walk-ins. Busy as Maryanne and Kerry both were, I noticed that Kerry worked longer hours. Maryanne was always booked solid without any gaps, but Kerry's appointments were more sporadic. While they were each taking home good incomes, Kerry worked harder and longer for her money than Maryanne because she was not trying to increase her average ticket sales. She was also not focused on getting the next appointment, also known as prebooking, which is why she worked six days a week instead of four days a week for the same money as Maryanne.

To calculate your average ticket sales number, you take the total for service sales that you brought in for the week and divide it by how many clients you served.

Let's go back to Maryanne: she would add extra revenue by giving clients highlights while they had a touch-up processing or offering them conditioning treatments or brow waxes, whatever services she could do *that benefited her clients* while increasing each sale and thereby maximizing her time in the salon. When I observed her discussing these additional services with her client, it was never pressured and always came off as casual conversation, not as a sales pitch. Kerry, on the other hand, was happy to do what the client asked and nothing more than she was supposed to do. To all appearances, Kerry was busy, but I can't imagine she was happy with those longer, harder hours. Maryanne's sales totals were usually higher than Kerry's, and she left the shop three hours earlier. Being busy is awesome, but being busy with the right type of client is better.

I noticed a big difference up at the front desk between Maryanne's clients and mine. The receptionist would always have a hard time helping Maryanne's clients get their next appointment because she was so busy. So her clients were routinely booking two appointments in advance out of fear of losing their spot to vacations and holidays and having to look at roots or go without their haircuts. My clients, on the other hand, when asked if they wanted to make their next appointments, would always say no; they would just call when they were ready or they didn't know their schedules—and then they wouldn't come back for three months. This led to another one of my lightbulb moments of basic economics: if you lessen your supply of time (because you're booked up), the demand for it goes up, just like with Maryanne's appointments. To put it another way, if you have a large supply of time, your demand goes down, as evidenced by my sad little empty appointment book.

Another thing I noticed was that most of her clients would absolutely not compromise on letting their hair go an extra week or two. They came in every five weeks or less like clockwork. So I began to do the math and realized what a gem these regular clients were. I began to think of them as the Elite Client. Later in this chapter, you can see the math and the difference in revenue produced from the ordinary client versus an elite client.

Now fast forward a few years to Evolutions. My clients don't leave now until they make at least one appointment, if not three or four. Elite clients really skyrocketed the growth of my business. Looking at the big picture, I found that the changes I needed to make were small, but they made a great impact on my clients.

We have also seen significant changes in the appointment books and in the paychecks of the stylists in my salon. Jessica, one of the newer stylists, came to work for me a year ago. When she left her former employer, her average sales week was just like mine had been, about $900 per week. Six months later, her average sales week was $1,600. She was able to accelerate the growth of her clientele and grow her weekly sales average by over 75 percent by using the elite client concept. And then, of course, her tips reflected the increased sales growth. Her goal is to be able to reach a steady $2,000 a week in service sales by her first-year anniversary with us. Jessica was able to significantly increase her average sales in a matter of months. I will show you how you can too.

The elite client concept covers simple, proven steps to increase your demand as a stylist. It is a conscious effort every day to benefit your own career and income. Each day, in one form or another, I am working to increase the demand on my appointment book because as long as the appointment book is full, I can be confident in the health of my business and my future income. So this is my story. I now have control of my career and my business, and now I am passing on to you the meat and potatoes of exactly how I did it. Let's get down to business.

First you'll need a few things

Before you can begin, you will need a notebook to track your totals for the next section and to measure your future progress. So go and get that now, please! You'll also want to have a calculator on hand so you can see your true numbers. You'll also need a pen and a marker, and lastly you will need a small box with blank index cards and ABC separators.

Don't be afraid to look stupid

Think of it this way: even when you work in someone else's salon, you are actually running your own business within their business. The product is your services, and the goal is to sell as many services to clients that will generate the most income for you. I consider all stylists who are paid on commission to be in business for themselves. So as a fellow business owner, I want to share the lessons that have had the most impact for me.

1. Don't be afraid to look stupid; it's the person that never tries to do anything better or different that looks really stupid.

2. By writing down your goals, you will make them seem much more easily obtainable. Include your final goal, as well as the steps you will need to complete the goal. (Spelling will never count here, and pictures or drawings are just fine.)

3. Tell a few other people your goals. You are a lot more likely to have success if you verbalize your aspirations to others, especially to people who will hold you accountable.

4. Embrace change. Your goals can change and evolve as you grow and expand your vision.

5. Absolutely EVERYTHING you do in your personal and professional life is a CHOICE!

GOAL SETTING

When Gretchen told me I should think about a managerial position, I was flattered and interested but also intimidated. I didn't believe I could ever reach that position, so I bolted. Evolutions was different; I couldn't run away. I was fully invested, my house was on the line, and my staff looked to me for their income; it absolutely had to work. My client Ginger had me put my personal and professional goals on paper, no matter how outrageous they seemed. It worked. By putting your goals in writing, they become a real possibility. Once they are in writing, they stay on your mind as long as you read them on a regular basis. You will consciously or even subconsciously begin to take small steps to make personal changes to achieve the goal that you desire. Originally Ginger told me to get a binder and put my goals in it under dividers labeled personal and professional. I tried that, but it did not work for me. The binder went onto a shelf, and I never looked at it again. I need things to be right in my face. My goals have to be big and bold, and I need to see them daily so I can be reminded what I am working for. I tend to be easily sidetracked.

I have five sheets of cardstock paper thumbtacked on my bedroom wall, labeled with each department of my life: Personal, Evolutions, this Book, and two other small businesses that I own. Each paper is divided with a line, with "long-term" and "short-term" written on either side. I keep things I can achieve within a year on the short-term side and big-picture goals on the other. Feel free to find your own way. Motivation that works is key.

Let's start by having you set up your own career goals. Find that notebook I mentioned earlier and have it handy, because you will have to update it daily. It's important that you are working toward things that truly motivate you. In large letters, write three goals with a marker on the outside cover of the notebook. Place the goals in the order that is most important to you. Be as specific about your goals as possible, but keep it short and direct. Think about where you would like to be in a year in each of these categories: More Money, More Free Time, and Steady Year-Round Income. You *need* to be able to glance at the cover of your notebook and know exactly what it says. Another way to frame the goal of **More Money** would be to use a concrete example like "$2,000 sales weekly by Sept." or "Take home $60,000 by Sept. next year." You could replace **More Free Time** with "Four days at home with the kids" or "Spend month in Italy next year." A **Steady Year-Round Income** really says it all, although add a projection date to give you your motivation.

NOTEBOOK 1ST ENTRY

Replace my goals written below with your own specific goals. Use your marker and put them right on the front cover of your notebook.

More Money

More Free Time

Steady Year-Round Income

HOW THE ELITE CLIENT CONCEPT WORKS (NOTEBOOK 2ND ENTRY)

Write the following on the inside top cover:

Step 1: Attract elite clients

Step 2: Prebook and create buzz for new referrals

Step 3: Increase average sales per ticket

Step 4: Scale back your hours

DEFINING THE ELITE CLIENT

We all have our favorite clients based on personality and (let's be honest) the size of their tips, but looking more closely at how and when the client books their appointment will tell you if they are the type of client you want.

Before you can book the right type of client, we need to categorize clients into groups. There are three types of clients:

Bad Clients

Good Clients

Elite Clients

Bad Clients arrive late or not at all; their appointments are sporadic throughout the year.

Good Clients arrive on time, but they don't prebook their appointments. They usually have good intentions of coming in every five weeks, but for whatever reason they don't.

Elite Clients **ALWAYS PREBOOK!** They always prebook their appointments every five weeks or less, and they usually have more than one service done at each visit.

If all you're getting are good and bad clients, not to worry; elite clients can evolve. As you book up and fewer appointments become available, the good clients that really love you will evolve into elite clients. The bad clients have less opportunity to get booked with you, so they will go to someone else, resulting in a lot fewer no-shows.

I love to hear my clients say, "Wow, you're really busy. I had to wait four weeks for this appointment." This is when I put on my poker face. "Oh yes, I'm sorry you had to wait so long, but I am booking six to seven weeks in advance. You know, I already have several days booked out already around the holiday, so if you can, you should prebook for the rest of the year." Inside I am smiling because my business is nice and healthy and I just created another elite client appointment booking.

Note book 3rd entry

On the inside cover under "Steps" (Attract, Prebook, Average, Scale back), write this quick outline about each type of client:

- *Bad—no-shows, late, no prebooking*

- *Good—no prebooking, six weeks or more*

- *Elite—<u>Always prebooks </u>every five weeks or less*

Why is prebooking so important?

Picture a small snowball rolling down a hill. It picks up a little snow and then a little more; now it's starting to gain some momentum. Pretty soon it's a very large, monstrous snowball. Think of your appointment book in the same way. Your first client books every five weeks and then another and another. Pretty soon you're fully booked, with many of them elite clients who are committing their money to you for the following month. You have essentially secured your own year-round income. The elite client is not a seasonal client; she comes every five weeks or so, no matter what.

Show me the money!

Let's say your average elite customer spends seventy dollars each visit in your salon for color and a cut. Here is the difference between prebooking her every five weeks and letting her go longer, say seven or even twelve weeks, just like a typical, good, nonprebooking client.

Example A	Rachel visits every 5 wks = 10 visits a year x $70 =	$700
Example B	Kathy visits every 7 wks = 7 visits a year x $70 =	$490
Example C	Meghan visits every 12 wks = 4 visits a year x $70 =	$280

The difference between Rachel, who comes in every five weeks, and Meghan, who visits every twelve weeks, is $420. That's a significant amount of money to lose on one client.

The tremendous loss in potential income to you becomes painfully clear when you multiply it by the number of clients for your projected **annual** total. For this example I used an average number of clients a regular stylist has, one hundred clients.

Example A	100 clients x $700 =	$70,000
Example B	100 clients x $490 =	$49,000
Example C	100 clients x $280 =	$28,000

The difference can really be seen now between example A and Example C: **$42,000** a year! **And this doesn't even take into account the difference in tips!**

Now let's get personal. It's time to run *your* actual numbers so we can make some financial goals for *you* for the upcoming year.

First, fill in what your usual average ticket price is below and do the math.

Example A	Dawn visits every 5 wks = 10 visits a year x $_____ =	$ _____
Example B	Vicki visits every 7 wks = 7 visits a year x $_____ =	$ _____
Example C	Meredith visits every 12 wks = 4 visits a year x $_____ =	$ _____

Next, figure out your totals by the year. Change the amount received from clients per year to what reflects your actual numbers. Just average it out if you don't know for sure.

Example A	_____ # of clients x $ _____ =	$_____
Example B	_____ # of clients x $ _____ =	$_____
Example C	_____ # of clients x $ _____ =	$_____

Take a look at the difference the yearly totals make. At first, it was almost unbelievable to me how much money I was losing just because of one or two weeks. Prebooking elite clients every five weeks really makes a huge difference to your total yearly sales. Every time you add an elite client to your client list, congratulate yourself because you are adding a significant amount of income to your yearly total.

We have a new hairstylist at the salon, named Lynn, who came into my shop fresh from the factory (beauty school). After a few months of training, she officially started on the floor. So essentially she has started with a weekly total of $0. But Lynn knows how to attract elite clients because I taught her myself, and she has proven to be a good student. Within ten weeks her total went from $0 to $860 for the week. I can't even tell you how ridiculous this seems to me. Lynn did in ten weeks what took me two years to do, even after all the training I had been given at Sassoon.

Example A will be your sales goal for this upcoming year. **You can only reach this goal by prebooking appointments!**

NOTEBOOK 4TH ENTRY

Find the total in Example A. Now under the client definitions (bad, good, elite) in your notebook, write

My sales goal total for this year is $_____.

RECAPPING THE MAIN POINTS

- *Real success and balance will be found only by booking elite clients.*

- *Specific goal setting will give you focus and keep you motivated .*

- *You set your personal goals.*

- *PREBOOK, PREBOOK, PREBOOK.*

- *You set your sales goal total for this year.*

Chapter Two

How to Attract the Desired Elite Client

In the beginning it definitely does take more effort to attract and keep elite clients. I have absolutely found it worth the time and effort, and I know you will too. Old habits die hard. This was the reason I took so long to get where I am today, but motivation from your personal goals and focusing on one or two changes a week will change your life and boost your career and income. Let's focus now on what *you* can do to build and sustain a desirable clientele.

STEP 1: ATTRACT ELITE CLIENTS

YOUR CLOTHES

The way I feel in my clothes is revealed by my attitude and energy level. If I look like crap, then that's the way I feel all day. Attracting the elite client means you need them to know that you take great care of yourself and will therefore do the same for them. I always try to aim for a level of style above my main goal clientele. People are drawn to successful-looking people because they want to be associated with them. Having your own personal dress code even if your salon does not enforce one will only help you feel successful.

Nice clothing gives you the best bang for your buck when you want people to see you as a successful person. And don't think you can separate out what you wear at home, in the neighborhood, from what you wear when you go to work: you never know who you will meet for the first time or who you'll run into, or where your next new elite client is going to come from.

I admit that I am critical and that I constantly pass judgment on my clients and make assumptions about them. I know they are in turn doing the same to me and my staff. At Evolutions I have a dress code of a black or neutral-colored dress pant and tailored shoes. Very simple, and we always look like we put time and thought into our outfits every day. My working wardrobe consists of four pairs of black dress pants and six shirts. I make sure all of the shirts are cut differently with their collars and textures so it doesn't look like I am wearing the same style each day. I always know that I match and really can't go wrong in any combination. I also always wear a bracelet, necklace, and earrings. I have sets in a black enamel, marcasite, silver, and gold. I change my accessories daily to give each outfit a different look. As far as my shoes, I prefer to wear heels because I feel like I look more professional and find I have more self-confidence because I look good. I also have a simple black leather heel, a fancier leather heel with more detail, and one set of flat Saturday shoes that are simple but professional looking.

When you are shopping, be sure that what you buy is age appropriate and not too sexy. Your clothes need to be tasteful, or you may unknowingly make a more conservative client uncomfortable. I avoid low-cut shirts or extremely short skirts and ask my staff to do so as well. Weed out your closet. If the clothes don't fit well, are dated, or need repair, take them out of the closet and attend to them. The bottom line is …

If you don't feel confident and successful in an outfit, you probably don't look it either. Take it off, and put on one you can feel successful in.

Don't worry what your co-workers say if you start coming in a little more pulled together, especially if you're doing this on your own. They will soon begin to see why, and after a while you may even have a few copycats.

WEAR WHAT YOU SELL!

If a stylist can't do her own hair and makeup nicely, why on earth would a client think the stylist will be able to do theirs? This is a really, really big deal. I am shocked by how many stylists I see who don't get this. They walk around with dark roots and faded hair color or roll out of bed and just throw their hair up in a claw clip and go to work. Makeup is just as important. We need to look as great and as fresh as possible every single day. No client wants to come in to a salon to get their hair done by someone who can't even pull it together themselves. You cannot expect to sell clients beauty routines, retail, or services with a look that says, "I don't do these things myself."

CONFIDENCE

Your personality and style can be seen in your energy level. The laws of attraction definitely apply here. The energy you put out will be drawn back to you. It is all about the presentation of *you*. Two hairstylists can do hair equally as well, but if one stylist barely makes eye contact and stands with her shoulders slumped over, I question that person's abilities. On the other hand, if a stylist is attentive to my needs and is a charismatic positive person, that stylist will certainly see me again. Positive energy acts like a people magnet. Be the magnet.

BODY LANGUAGE

Every once in a while I still get a little nervous doing someone's hair, but I never want to show it. Maintaining a good posture and making eye contact exudes confidence to the client. It lets the client know you are present, listening, and attentive to their needs. Be aware of how you look to the client. Keep your arms uncrossed and hands out of your pockets when consulting; otherwise, it will come across that you're judgmental or even perplexed. Slumped shoulders look weak. Poor body language will make clients nervous and give them a reason to second-guess your competence and abilities.

CONVERSATION

Speaking with clients was the hardest part for me when I first started on the floor. I didn't know what to say, especially to new clients whose age bracket was different from my own. Originally I just asked them questions and let them do all the talking Are you married? Where do you live? Have you lived there a long time? Do you have children? Where were you having your hair done? This was okay for the first visit, but I had nothing to talk about during the second visit because I couldn't remember anything that they had said. I still ask these questions to keep new clients engaged in conversation; I just don't ask all of them during the same visit. Eventually I began to smarten up by keeping a card on each client, even the clients that did not receive chemical services. I could quickly refresh my memory and be ready to make the client comfortable and the conversation engaging. This is why you need those index cards.

Example of information on index card

Gwyneth Smith   555-5555
Referral from Eva Rubin (ex-sister-in-law)
123 Vincent St Babylon, NY
2 Boys, 1 Girl
First visit 1/1/2008

Even if you don't remember this client because you're now so busy, you'll have something to open the conversation with. So, how are those kids these days? Has the ex been behaving? Did you see the beautiful house being built by the Dukes around the bend from you? Doesn't it look amazing?

Everyone's only interested in one thing!

We are all human. And we are all genuinely interested in the exact same thing, *ourselves.* So be sure to keep the conversation directed at the person who is *paying for the time in your chair.* This means not the other stylists, not your assistant, not the other stylist's clients, no one but the client paying for your time at that moment. Keep the conversation interesting for the client by continually turning the conversation back to them. This will keep them engaged and ensure that they are having a good time. If you are like me and become nervous, don't worry about it; they are so busy talking they won't even notice. Clients will, of course, want to get to know you, too. Fine. Keep it positive and short. "Oh, yes, Tim is great. He just started to get the boat ready to go in the water. We are looking into going to the Jersey shore for a week this summer. Weren't you there last year?" Save your sob story for your therapist; truthfully, clients don't want to hear it, and they don't really care about your problems. The only thing your complaining will do is bring the client down—not the mood you want them leaving your chair with. The bottom line is …

> *Clients are just secretly praying that your issues aren't affecting the quality of the service you're providing them.*

Topics of conversation

Here are some topics that almost never fail to keep conversation flowing:

celebrity news

local news

sports teams

fashion designers

television shows, especially award shows and reality TV

Ask your client's opinion about anything; people love to give advice. Ask them about the new water park or vacation spot that they just went to and if it would be age appropriate for your kids. Ask their opinion about the new outlet center that just opened by their home. Ask them for the best route they take to the airport since they fly all the time. It doesn't matter what you talk about; just keep your conversation appropriate.

You should absolutely NEVER discuss your financial situation, good or bad, with a client. It is unprofessional and makes clients feel uncomfortable and even potentially obligated to leave a larger tip than they would have otherwise (if you weren't crying the blues). Religion and politics are also big topics to avoid, as they spark too much debate and you could risk losing a client if your opinions differ.

Education

A great topic of conversation is your education. Yes, clients love hearing about the latest hair show you went to. Just knowing that you went will make you seem in the know, on the cutting edge, and it will boost your professional credibility in your client's eyes. Extra bonus: When clients hear that something is new or fashionable, it makes it more appealing. Your client may therefore LOVE to try a new color or haircut based on what you just learned at the latest class or show. What's even better than the increased ticket? The style change will create more attention for your client and will result in more referral opportunities for you.

RECAPPING THE MAIN POINTS

- *Don't feel successful in an outfit? Take it off!*

- *If you can't do your own hair, why should a client trust you to do theirs?*

- *Positive energy acts like a people magnet.*

- *Bad body language lets people second-guess your competence.*

- *The conversation needs to be directed at the client paying for your time.*

Chapter Three

Taking Care of Your Elite Clients

The elite client has arrived ... Now what?

I have seen stylists treat their client like cattle. You can almost hear them holler, "Next!" The elite client won't come back if you're just herding them in; they expect a higher level of attention and a better quality of service. Don't disappoint them.

Notebook 5th entry

Under your sales goals for the year, write the summary below:

The Elite Client Checklist

1. **Greet!** Greet the client by name.

2. **Consult!** Consult before the shampoo.

3. **Like!** When you're done, make sure they like their hair.

4. **Thank!** Thank the client for coming in.

5. **Prebook!** Bring them to the desk and ask them to book their next appointment.

GREET!

You should know your client's name and what they are coming in for before they arrive. This is a detail you will need your front desk to take care of. When it's not your salon and this (or anything else you would like to change) is something you wish to do, just ask! Your salon doesn't want to risk losing a rainmaker—you! At Evolutions, our receptionist walks over to the stylist and explains quietly that the client has arrived, her name, the services to be provided, and the time of the appointment. If this isn't an option, you could ask for a printout of your schedule when you first get in and have it updated if it changes, or perhaps you or the receptionist could copy down the schedule. You will need to judge what will work best based on the salon.

When you greet your client, it should always be by name: "Hi, Maureen, how are you today? I have you down for a cut and color. Is that right? Great; lets get you comfortable in a color chair, and I will be right with you."

CONSULT!

Consulting with the client before their hair is washed or you mix their color lets them know you are listening to them and not rushing though their service. I am not just talking about new clients. You need to consult the client that has been with you even years. A thorough consult will reduce the potential number of clients who do not return because they were unhappy with their hair or felt otherwise rushed. Never, never premix your color before you first consult with the client. This might be the day your long-term client wants to change.

What color is this?

When discussing color, speak in descriptive words to make them seem more appealing and flattering to the client:

- *Beach blonde*

- *Honey blonde*

- *Strawberry blonde*

- *Copper red*

- *Soft caramel brown*

- *Chocolate brown*

- *Dark rich brown*

Do the same when discussing cuts or styles:

- *Frame the face with angles.*

- *Accentuate the cheekbones with long bangs.*

- *Open up your face by lifting the length away from the jawline.*

- *Create more movement through the hair with layers.*

This gives the client a customized look and feel that only you can provide for them!

Do you even know what you're talking about?

You need to sound informed. The idea of knowing everything about every product available, and when and why—and on what hair type—it's best used, makes my brain hurt. You are selling *services*. Your clients just want someone to take charge, to put a plan in place to get them where they want to go. Map it out for them; tell them, "Today this is the service you need and here's why." Just knowing a few details about the most popular products you sell will lift your sales and increase the confidence a client has in your care.

Here are two of my favorite scripts:

1. On color: "Since you are trying to cover 100 percent gray hair, a derivative of ammonia needs to be in every formula for it to work. That's why you're not getting very good coverage at home with those boxes of wash in temporary color. Once you try our color, you will see a big difference." Presto! You have yourself a new elite color client.

2. On highlights: "I think your hair is breaking because your stylist is leaving the bleach on for too long and overlapping it onto the ends. Our bleach has a blue-violet base that tones at the same time it lifts, so it doesn't need as long to work." Voila! Here's a new elite highlight client.

Sounds like I know what I'm talking about, right? I do, but I don't know anything specific about the other chemicals or ingredients in these products, except for what I've already said.

Promises, promises

Here is where you need to be careful. You want the client to have confidence in your abilities, but you don't want to overpromise and then have the client leave feeling disappointed. The bottom line is ...

Underpromise and overdeliver

Elite clients will sing your praises. If your client has unrealistic expectations, you need to change them or you will have a redo on your hands. Clients need to know before the service begins what to expect. This is *especially* true for new clients. I like to work backward. I do not care where you used to go three years ago, who your hairdresser was, or what your hairstyle was in 1972. All I want to know is where are you going, whether it is twenty minutes from now or a year from now. It's my job to design the plan of how to get you there. If I tell a client, "It will take me three appointments to get you where you want to go," I would like to exceed their expectation by doing it in two appointments.

Within my first year on the floor, I got a new client in my chair, Rachel. Rachel had been dyeing her hair black for several years with a home care product. Now she wanted to be light blonde *today*. "Sure, no problem," I said and went to mix the bleach. At this point Maryanne gave me a look through the mirror at what I had just promised this client and quickly followed me into the back room. She told me there was no way in hell I was ever going to get that girl blonde today and I had better fix her expectations fast. Gotta love Maryanne! She was right, of course. So I went back out there and explained to Rachel that there would be no blonde today but I could do light brown. So she went home light brown that day and came back the next month for highlights, and she was very happy. You need to make sure that the clients' expectations are in line with what you can actually deliver for them. Most don't expect miracles and rely on you to tell them honestly what is and what isn't going to work.

When to say NO

I would never recommend a service to a client that wasn't right for them just to make an extra buck. Great stylists know when to say no. No to doing a service that they know will wreck the clients' hair, and no to a client who refuses to listen to what you are trying to tell them. It's rare to have to say no, but don't be afraid to say it, because it's *your* reputation on the line.

Last year a client of five years came to see me. Vicki is a stay-at-home mom with three small children. Our conversation during previous visits always centered around how expensive preschool was, along with all the extra activities the older children were doing after school—karate, ballet, soccer, and gymnastics. That day she announced she'd decided to go blonde. Vicki had naturally dark brown hair, so you can imagine it was going to be expensive and time-consuming to maintain. I let her down gently by itemizing the cost of maintaining this hair color over the course of a year. It wasn't that

I didn't want to do it or couldn't do it, but I knew the expense was going to catch up to her and she would end up throwing on a box color to save money. (I will also admit that I didn't want everyone at the PTA being told I do her hair.) Tactfully I told her all of this. She saw my point right away, and she is still a brunette.

A potential client named Carla came into the shop when I first went on the floor. I say potential because I had to flat out refuse to do her hair. When she checked in at our front desk, I could tell she was not a salon regular, not at our salon or anyone else's for that matter. She was in my appointment book for just a perm. I brought her to my chair rather than bringing her back to the sink where we usually consulted a perm client. I needed to find out what her expectations were. She had been using home care color for the past several years in different shades of gold, orange, and brown, and she told me she had not had a haircut in over a year, which was pretty easy to see since she had a lot of split ends. But today Carla wanted a perm, and that was it. She was also firm that her husband liked long hair. The condition of her hair was bad, especially the last three inches, which I knew would not hold up to being permed. Carla refused to get a haircut! I looked at her ends again, took a deep breath, and told her I could not do a perm without cutting her hair because of the condition of the ends. She refused, saying again she only wanted the perm. I glanced at Maryanne at this point since her chair was right next to mine. Maryanne gave me a quick nod to say no. "Sorry," I said to Carla, "I won't be able to help you."

My reputation is more important than any income I would have gotten from doing this woman's perm. I didn't realize it at the time, but it was a great lesson.

Details

The elite client wants to know that they are receiving a more personable service than they can get down the block. Here is where the details matter. Clients may not say anything, but they know when you're cutting corners, and then they just don't come back to you. Taking a little more time to polish those ends smooth with the dryer, or having them stand up for the haircut when the hair is below the chair, matters. This is a truly personalized service, and this is why they will come back.

It's in the details …

- *Have all of your supplies cleaned, prepped, and ready to go for each client when they arrive.*

- *Be sure clients have their legs uncrossed when you're cutting to avoid an uneven cut.*

- *Section properly and take extra time to recheck lines of a haircut.*

- *Go back over the front hairline after a touch-up is done to clean the skin of color.*

- *Make sure they are comfortable with coffee and magazines before you leave them to process.*

- *Give specialized instructions to the shampoo person of the right products to use.*

- *Ask the client what type of product they put in their hair, and if you have a better option, tell them.*

- *Take the time to make sure the product you use for the blowout is thoroughly massaged through the hair.*

- *Be a perfectionist; make sure your haircuts are even and look the best they can.*

- *Put down any flyaways before the client leaves.*

The bottom line is ...

Do whatever it is that makes your services better than anyone else's and do it consistently for each and every client.

Tools

Your blow-dryer, bushes, hot irons, flat irons, and so on should always be in excellent working order. The dryer you use should be a professional one, along with all your other heat styling tools. It doesn't look professional to use cheap brand names or weak wattage equipment and expect people to pay a good price for your services. Brushes and combs should be completely clean and free of hair for each and every client, and if you drop them on the floor, they need to be cleaned right away. Make sure the client sees you taking care of your tools. Nothing angers me more than watching a stylist take a dirty brush full of other people's hair and begin styling a client. I would not blame the client if they didn't return.

LIKE!

When things are said out loud, it makes them more real. Ask the client, "Do you like your hair?" You want them to acknowledge that they like it out loud. In the rare case that they don't like it, you can quickly rectify the problem while they are still in the salon, instead of giving them the opportunity to tell family and friends how much they don't like your work.

I knew that Jessica, now one of my top stylists at Evolutions, was a keeper after a very difficult first week. A new color client, Francesca, came in on Jessica's fourth day. One of my habits in the salon is to eavesdrop on my staff's consultations with their clients. I want to know what the client is asking for and to see what kind of service they receive from my staff. I listened intently to the details of this consultation, and I continuously glanced through my mirror to the two of them involved in conversation. I began to feel my entire body be overwhelmed with heat. Then I really began to sweat. Francesca, dark haired and olive skinned, was ready for a total change. She wanted the five-inch section between the nape of her neck and her occipital bone made a very light blond and then on the top have the same light blonde and black foiled through the rest in a bold chunky pattern. I realized I had not spoken to Jessica about doing creative work, and I had no idea if she could even handle this complicated type of service. I had to consciously tell myself to breath. Inhale … exhale … inhale …

Jessica seemed confident, and she had a fairly quick consultation with Francesca. What first impressed me was Jessica's patience as she foiled her with forty volume and bleach almost solidly on the bottom and then did the top, taking her time to get it laid out the way the client wanted it. I was anxious the entire time, but I held myself back from getting involved. Jessica brought her up to a beautiful light blonde, and she came out great. After Francesca was toned, cut, and blown dry, after looking at it in the mirror a few minutes, she mentioned that she would have liked to have the blonde absolutely solid on the underneath when she pulled her hair back. Rather than have her client go out unhappy, Jessica took responsibility right away, realizing she should have asked her about that during the consultation.

Jessica took Francesca back to the color area to remedy the situation and make her client happy. After another round of bleach, toner, and blow-drying, she had finished Francesca's hair—and it was awesome. Francesca loved it. You could just tell; she was positively radiant. Jessica was happy her client was happy, and I could finally breathe normally again. Everything was great until Jessica removed Francesca's gown. In my head all I could think of was "Oh F**K!" Francesca's gray sweater was now a bleached and spotted mess. The gown had absorbed some of the bleach during the second trip to the sink. Without losing her poise, Jessica alerted Francesca to the problem and acquired the necessary information to replace the sweater for her. The accountability that Jessica assumed paid off tenfold. Because of her professionalism, Francesca is now a loyal monthly client and has currently referred Jessica eleven other customers in just this year alone.

What to do when a client doesn't like their look

Let's say the client leaves and calls back the next day because they don't like their new style. This happens occasionally, and how you handle it will set you apart. Ask the client to come in so you can see the problem. Most likely you will realize you missed something in the original consultation or that the application was lacking. If the client was the one who didn't explain herself properly, it is still your fault because you didn't give a thorough enough consultation. *Never* place blame on the client. Acknowledge the mistake, get a plan ready to fix the problem, and do it. Call the color company if you need to, or ask for a coworker's opinion. You are giving the customer confidence when they feel very vulnerable, and once you correct the problem, you will end up with a loyal client and plenty of referrals.

THANK!

Thank the clients for letting you do their hair. It lets them know you appreciate them and their patronage. Clients have lots of options and other places they can take their business. Thanking them for coming in is a simple thing to do, and it has such a positive impact.

PREBOOK!

Keeping your appointment book full at all times maximizes your time in the salon. Waiting around from one appointment to the next is just wasting your time. Remember that small snowball rolling down the hill? To keep your appointment book full, you'll want to create a sense of urgency. People act quickly if there is a fear of losing out. This can be the best motivator to quickly build and grow your elite clientele.

To see what I mean, sit down and watch a home shopping network for ten minutes. Just by hearing there are only twenty items of such and such left and they won't have this product again for six months makes you begin to really want that product. Similarly, a sense of urgency can be created until you really are fully booked by elite clients. To do this, tell them to secure their next appointment before they leave because (fill in the blank— prom season, a holiday, your vacation, their vacation) is coming up and the time they will want will go quickly. I no longer even have to tell my clients to prebook appointments; they do it automatically. More and more of my elite clients have gone way beyond booking five weeks ahead and have booked for the entire year. Soon yours will too! The bottom line is …

PREBOOK ALL YOUR CLIENTS!

Checking out the client

1. Walk your client up to the desk, and itemize the services she had to your receptionist. "Okay, Andrea, today Ginger had a full highlight, a root touch-up, and a haircut." By itemizing the services, you create added value for the customer. Ginger knows I did a lot of work on her hair today, and it helps justify the price when Andrea tells her the bill.

2. "Ginger, you won't need highlights again for a while, but you will need a root touch-up and trim in five weeks. Let's set up your next appointment today because your next visit falls really close to the holiday week, and you know we're always packed. Andrea, please book Ginger for the first week in November. She prefers to come in after 6 p.m. Is that good, Ginger?"

I already know that Ginger needs an evening appointment, and she will have the feeling that I am really taking great care of her, setting up her next appointment—and I am, but I am taking care of me too!

Reception area

You can control the prebooking while the client is in the salon, but the receptionist controls the calls coming in. She or he is, therefore, a very powerful member of your team, and the right relationship can make or break your weekly sales total and income. You need to be very kind to your receptionist. Explain your goals and the role that they will have in the success of your career (preferably over a lunch that you are paying for).

The most important task for the reception desk, next to collecting payments, is to know how to efficiently book clients. The receptionist should always try to book clients in the first appointment space that is open. Here is a little reception desk makeover:

Receptionist: "Thank you for calling Evolutions Hair Salon, Andrea speaking. How may I help you?"

Client: "This is Ellen Shapiro. I wanted to book an appointment for Saturday morning with either Jonathan or Lucas for a highlight and haircut."

Receptionist. "Okay, let me take a look. You know, Jonathan actually just had a cancellation for that same service this evening, I could get you in tonight at 5 p.m. if you like."

Client. "That sounds great. It clears my weekend. Let me take that appointment."

That same receptionist could have just stuck her in on Saturday morning and done her job, but putting that extra effort into the appointment booking just doubled the possibilities of your sales. This client will come in and pay for her services tonight, and the chances are high that the desirable Saturday appointment will be taken by someone else. You will now be collecting double the money.

Your receptionist can create demand!

If your receptionist tells a client that you have "no availability" at the time that he or she wants, rather than "she doesn't come in till 4 p.m.," the impression she is giving clients is that you are in *high* demand.

When a client calls to make an appointment and asks what is open, you will want your receptionist to automatically ask the client instead what time of day they are looking for. When she knows whether it is a morning, afternoon, or night appointment, *then* she should offer the options. "Afternoon, okay, I have a 1:30 open." The receptionist can diminish the value and demand on a stylist's appointment book when she acts like a drone: "okay, I have 11:00 a.m., 1:30 p.m., 2:30 p.m., 3 p.m., 4:30 p.m., 6 p.m., and a 6:30 p.m." Too much availability (supply) for the client, and not enough perception of demand for the stylist.

Your waitlist

As you grow your elite clientele and your appointments become less available, tell your receptionist to keep a waitlist for you at especially busy times of the year like Christmas and August for back-to-school clients. I usually have anywhere from three to five people waiting for an appointment. Without fail, something changes daily on my schedule—people cancel or someone is sick. Andrea, my receptionist, can usually get another client in the time slot before I even know that I had a cancellation, and then I don't have to lose any money.

RECAPPING THE MAIN POINTS

- *Greet, consult, like, thank, prebook.*

- *Underpromise and overdeliver.*

- *Do what makes your services better, and do it consistently.*

- *Be kind to your receptionist.*

Chapter Four

Taking Care of You and Your Bottom Line

Chapters two and three are the longest in this guide because it takes effort to attract and keep the elite client, but by attracting these clients, it is easier to take care of yourself. Chapter four is all about taking care of you and making sure you are getting the most money you can for each hour you are in the salon. We will work on continually increasing your average sales per client so you can spend less time in the salon while still making the same income or even better. Finally, I want to show you how to use your notebook—the most important tool you have. Earlier we discussed step 1: attract elite clients. Now we're ready to move on and learn how to leverage your results.

STEP 2: PREBOOK AND CREATE BUZZ FOR NEW REFERRALS

REFERRALS ARE HOW YOU GROW

When clients recommend other potential clients to you, they are taking a chance. The new customer is judging you and is also judging the taste of the original client. If you get a good review after the first referral, you allow the client to feel comfortable referring people all the time without worry.

First impressions are very important, especially when you are building your elite clientele, and even when you're not on the job. People seeing you out in public or even just wanting to compliment on your look can spark a potential client to approach you. You *need* to carry preprinted business cards at all times. You want it to be as easy as possible for clients to do business with you. There is too much competition out there to let an interested customer just walk away without a way to find you.

If your salon does not provide you with business cards, find a printer and have your own made. The cards should include your name, the name of your salon, the address, the phone number, and your days and hours. Typically these can be done inexpensively: you can order 500 cards for about $40, and you will recoup that in no time.

In our salon we tracked our advertising dollars for one year and concluded that it costs about $125 to get a new client into the salon. On average, half stay with the salon, so now the cost to the salon is actually $250 in advertising dollars for each new client. That is why your referrals are so important. They are like freebies. After seeing the results of this study, we completely changed how we advertise. We stopped newspaper and magazine advertisements completely and turned our customers into walking advertisements.

Here's how our referral program works

Business cards are given to client #1 when they leave. There is a space for that client to sign their name.

When client #1 refers client #2, they give them the card. Client #2 comes in for a service and receives $5 off their service. Client #1 comes back in again for their next service and receives $5 off their service.

We have more than doubled our new clients per month. We also have a giveaway for the client that gives us the most referrals in a quarter. We used to do hotel stays and spa packages. When we asked clients for ideas, all they wanted were gift certificates to our salon. The cost per new customer is now less than a fifth of what it used to be!

Overbooking

If you respect your clients' time, they will respect yours. Being constantly behind is a horrible state to be in. You never feel in control of your day. If you need more time for a haircut, tell the receptionist it is her job to book you properly. It is far more important to give one great service to a satisfied client rather than two mediocre services to unhappy clients. If squeezing in clients is an option, remember that the client won't remember the favor of you squeezing them in but they will remember the bad haircut. Make sure you have enough time to do a great job.

STEP 3: INCREASE YOUR AVERAGE SALES PER TICKET

YOUR MOST VALUABLE TOOL IS YOUR NOTEBOOK!

This notebook will become your most valuable tool for your future. It will give you a financial snapshot of the information you need to know in order to justify a raise, increase your prices, or decide when to take your vacation.

You must keep your notebook in a very visible place for two reasons:

1. To read your personal goals on the cover every day and keep them fresh in your mind. Remember:

More Money

More Free Time

Steady Year-Round Income

NOTEBOOK 6TH ENTRY

2. To remember to enter in your numbers.

These need to be tracked daily:

- *The date*

- *The amount of service sales you do*

- *Hours spent in salon*

- *How many clients serviced*

- *Tips*

These need to be tracked weekly:

- *Your income*

- *Your average sales ticket*

The stylist in the following example is paid on a 50/50 commission:

Date	Sales	Hours	Clients	Tips
1/1	closed	0	0	$0
1/2	$213	8	4	$35
1/3	$275	8.5	5	$45
1/4	$175	6.5	3	$30
1/5	$321	8	6	$65
Total	**$984**	**31**	**18**	**$175**

Notes:

1. Weekly income = 50% of $984 = **$492**

2. Total gross pay before taxes = income $492 + tips $175 = **$667**

3. Average sales ticket = sales of $984 /18 clients = **$55 your average sale per client**

51

It's time to start setting up your notebook. Start on the first page and follow this model. Don't forget: you *must track daily* what your sales are to be able to see accurate progress.

Date	Sales	Hours	Clients	Tips
Total				

Notes:

1. Weekly income =

2. Total gross pay before taxes = income _____ + tips _____ =

3. Average sales ticket = sales of $_____ / _____ clients = $ _____ **your average sale per client**

At the end of each week and at the end of each month, it is time to compare numbers. The goals that you set— higher income and fewer work hours—will determine what numbers you care about. The category names below should be written at the end of every month and then again at the end of the year for your yearly total.

Average weekly total
Average sales per client

Hours spent in salon

Boost your average sales per client

Let's work on boosting your average sales per customer, otherwise known as upselling clients who are already in the shop. This will raise your average ticket price per customer and increase the value of your time. Boosting your tickets does not mean shoving retail products or extra services down your client's throat every time they come in. The proper way to do this is very casually. Try to sell whatever it is—a conditioning treatment or a new lighter flat iron—as an upgrade or a way to fix a problem, but don't get pushy. You want this to be as casual as possible and the exchange to be as friendly as possible so you make the client feel bad for saying no. This is always a great way to set up a sale for the next appointment, and it may be something the client was thinking of doing anyway and will be happy you suggested it.

Try these …

"I really like the base color we have been using, but I think it would look great with some highlights for the summer. What do you think?"

"A few of my customers who have fair skin like yours love the new sensitive wax that we have. If you would ever like to try it, let me know."

"Your next appointment is in September. Would you like to also book an appointment for an end-of-summer conditioning treatment to hydrate the ends before I do your haircut?"

Take advantage of special occasions

Special occasions open a short window of opportunity where a lot of clients disregard their budgets. The main concern of most clients is to look and feel great on that special day. Clients try services they have never used before, and they will book appointments well in advance leading up to the event, creating more demand for you. I really like special occasions because my clients have never looked better.

Step 4: Scale back hours

If you are new in the business or are not as busy as you would like to be, you need to pay your dues. Any available hours you have to work should be spent in the salon trying to get every walk-in or every last-minute client that calls for an appointment. As you become established and you see your appointment book fill up consistently (not just at peak season), you will want to further increase your demand by *scaling back your hours*. If you are booked for 75 percent of the week at least three to five weeks in advance, then you are ready to begin scaling back your hours. Take your slowest times first, an hour here or an hour there, just enough to compact the appointments in your book a little bit. You will want to start doing this six weeks in advance. You should always be working on all of the steps all the time, but now is when you need to really focus on step 3: increase your average sales per ticket.

Give yourself a few weeks to get used to the reduced hours. If you are able to steadily increase average ticket prices to compensate for the reduced hours, then reduce your hours some more. Repeat the cycle to meet your goals. If your weekly totals are not at least steady with what your service sales were before you scaled back your hours, then your appointment book was probably not at a high enough capacity of elite clients yet and it was premature to scale back your hours.

CELEBRATE YOUR TALENTS

Clients come to us to get their needs met, but they stay because we create an experience for them. This is what the best stylists and salons excel at, creating a total experience for the client. Celebrate what you are good at, whether it is cutting curly hair or giving exceptional blow-dries—and using *Trade Secrets of the Successful Hairstylist* will bring your career to a whole new level. People will pay more and wait longer for the experience of just getting an appointment with you.

Celebrate your talents. If you are excellent at color, sell that; if you are a fantastic up-do stylist, celebrate it. You will have more success with a few great talents and celebrating those rather than trying to do everything and being mediocre. And let people know what you are great at. You can do this without sounding obnoxious just as long as you say it with passion.

"Oh, Amy's prom is coming up. I am really great at doing up-do's; it is what I love to do. The girls always look so beautiful when their hair is done. Let me give you my card. I work right down the block. Bring her in any time for a free consultation with me, and you can look at my portfolio."

The bottom line is …

Celebrate your talents with a passion, and you will be fully booked in no time!

DISCOUNTS DO NOT REPLACE TALENT

A discount cannot take the place of focusing on a talent. You lose value and credibility when you are concerned solely with offering the best price. That kind of a client is a bargain shopper, and if a better price comes along, I bet you they will be gone in a flash. Who really wants to continually devalue their services to keep clients coming in anyway? The stylist will always end up being the loser. The best way that I can advise you to value yourself is education—take advanced education classes, and then make sure that the clients know about it. This enhances the value of your services and what you have to offer to clients.

If you feel strongly that the shop where you currently work is not going in the direction you want, it is time to get an exit plan together and change salons. Yes, I know all you discount salon owners will not like hearing this. Sorry, but the cycle of trying to make ends meet and trying to keep good staff is tough, especially since bargain prices do not leave much money for salaries. If you want to change this dynamic, start investing time and money into your employees. Once you have provided your staff with free education classes, their clients will see a difference in the quality of services, and you can slowly begin to break the clients out of their bargain habits. Some clients may not stay, but if changes are implemented slowly and thoughtfully, the salon will survive and can evolve into an elite salon.

IMPROVE YOUR INTERVIEWING SKILLS

If your goal is improving your work environment and you're looking to join a higher-quality salon, the most important thing you need to remember is that you are selling yourself. Just like the elite client likes to talk about herself, the salon owner is also self-interested and wants to know, "What's in it for me?" We want to know what you're going to bring to the table. I want to see energy, a willingness to learn, and confidence. Having an established clientele isn't everything. Things to do before the interview include:

- *Be nice as well as articulate to the receptionist when you call for the interview, as she is the gatekeeper to getting an interview. At Evolutions, if Andrea doesn't like you, then you won't see me.*

- *Don't get lost and risk being late for your appointment. Go to the salon the day before.*

- *Arrive at the interview no more and no less than ten minutes early.*

- *Make sure your hair and makeup are done (no roots).*

- *Don't drink coffee or smoke before the interview (gross!).*

At the interview:

- *Have a positive attitude.*

- *Make eye contact.*

- *Do your homework. You need to be able to say something honest and appropriate about the salon to the person interviewing you. Mention what a great reputation it has, or that you are impressed by the stylists' work because your neighbor goes there. Mention how modern the salon looks. Do your homework—it works!*

- *Bring photos of your work, even if you're fresh from beauty school.*

- *Show me a completely filled out resume with references (SPELL-CHECKED).*

- *Dress professionally head to toe (see "Your clothes" in chapter two).*

- *Don't bring any food, drink, or gum into the salon.*

  YOU'RE HIRED!

Recapping the main points

- *Freebie referrals are awesome.*

- *Your notebook is your most valuable tool.*

- *Increasing your average sales per client gives you more free time out of the salon.*

- *Further increase demand by scaling back your hours.*

- *Celebrate your talents.*

EAT OR BE EATEN

With our struggling economy, personal-service-based industries are at a crossroads. Some will go out of business as the number of clients able to afford salon services shrinks. This reality should remind you more than ever of the importance of treating your clients well and continuing to secure new clients in order to grow your income. The elite client is more stable than your average customer, but they expect a higher quality of service. By following the steps I've outlined in *Trade Secrets of the Successful Hairstylist*, you can build your clientele into an elite one and achieve your personal and professional goals even in a recession. My salon has been blessed to have achieved a 36 percent increase in our 2008 sales over 2007, and I was able to continue to cut my hours at the same time. I know it is solely because of my salon's effort and commitment to attracting elite clients.

As you reach the milestones that are important to you in achieving your goals, don't just let them pass by. Celebrate your achievements with people that care about you. You will deserve their congratulations—and treasure your new life of freedom and choices. You will be amazed at what is in store for you.

MORE MONEY

MORE FREE TIME

STEADY YEAR-ROUND INCOME

Share Your Success!

www.The-Successful-Hairstylist.com